causelife

causelife

water equals life

vernon brewer & noel brewer yeatts

with dc bowden

BOOKS

Published by World Help, Inc
Forest, Virginia

World Help
1148 Corporate Park Drive
Forest, VA 24551

worldhelp.net

contents

"Water is the sleeping giant issue of the 21st century and we all need to wake up about it."[1]

—Robert Redford

introduction

Clean water is essential for life.

But why are there so many people who do not have access to clean water?

When viewed from space, our planet looks like a blue marble. Seventy-one percent of its surface is covered with water.[2] Everyone on earth should have more than enough water to survive with plenty leftover!

However, only 3 percent of the water on earth is fresh and drinkable. From this very small amount of consumable fresh water, nearly 69 percent is locked up in glaciers and ice caps. This is not a very efficient or accessible source of clean water. But 30 percent is right under our feet. That means that 30 percent of the earth's fresh water can only be accessed by drilling.[3]

We must drill, because we need that water.

Most of us are aware that our body is approximately 60 percent water. But did you know that your brain is 70 percent water and your lungs are 90 percent?

Even blood is 83 percent water.[4]   If we do not have a supply of clean water, we cannot live.

You and I could survive weeks without food and in some cases maybe longer. But we can only survive eight to ten days without water. Each day we must replace 2.5 quarts of water.[5]

These are numbers we rarely think about through the course of our day or our lives. I think the reason we don't is because we don't have to.

I know these numbers weren't real for me until I experienced firsthand the suffering of those who did not have clean water in an African village. It was where my journey for providing clean water began over 20 years ago.

There was a famine in Africa with thousands starving to death in the Sudan and Ethiopia. The world was uniting to do something to help, and I had been on the sidelines far too long.

I had just survived a nearly two-year battle with cancer. My immune system was weak, which made me susceptible to colds, the flu, and every other disease. I still felt like life was passing me by and I had to make up for lost time. I just knew I had to do something.

After arriving in Nairobi, Kenya, we chartered a small, single-engine plane and flew north past the equator to the Sudan border and landed on a gravel runway. In the distance, I could see a village of grass huts. I had never seen a village like that before, except in *National Geographic*. So of course, I was intrigued.

As we got off the plane, it was over 100 degrees. The unbearable heat and humidity took our breath away. We were met by our African partner, and I asked him if we had time to visit the village.

Because of the famine and drought, there was no fresh water anywhere. I was told large trucks had to bring water in every day from as far away as 80 kilometers. It was sobering to see tribal women on their knees, digging with their bare hands in dry riverbeds, trying to find water. My friend said, "They won't find any water, but if they do, it will probably be contaminated and do them more harm than good."

We arrived at the village only to find it deserted—not a soul in sight. I began taking photos, snooping around, and even went up to one of the huts. It didn't have a door, only an opening with an animal skin covering. I stuck my head in to look around and was shocked to see a little girl, maybe 9 years old, standing just inside in the doorway. All she was wearing was a dirty pair of under-pants. She was filthy! Her hair was matted, her nose run-ning, and her belly distended—showing early signs of malnutrition. She had open sores all over her body and the smell was awful. All I could think about was my doc-tors' parting words, "Be careful what you touch." I was so repulsed; I took a giant step back and froze.

But then I thought, "Wait just a minute. Who do you think you are? Do you see that little girl? God loves her just as much as He loves your girls back home . . . and He has asked you to love her too." I was immediately humbled.

Partly out of guilt and partly out of impulse, I reached forward and picked up that dirty, smelly little girl and held her tight in my arms. I later found out I was the first white person she had ever seen, so I'm sure I scared her to death. I couldn't speak her language and she couldn't speak mine. But I held her, touched her cheek, and tried my best to show her I cared.

What happened next is still hard to believe after all these years. While I was holding that dirty, destitute child, out from the hut came her mother, father, brothers, and sisters, and even her grandparents. I didn't realize so many people could fit inside one hut. Not only did the hut empty out, but within minutes, I was surrounded by everyone in the village—several hundred starving and thirsty nomadic Turkana Africans.

I saw an elderly woman who was blind, a man with a tumor on his neck—obviously terminal—and another man whose leg was swollen three or four times its normal size. I looked into the eyes of the diseased, blind, and lame. For the first time in my life, I realized what Jesus must have felt when he saw the crowds and *"was moved with compassion for them."*[6]

I felt so helpless in the face of such great human suffering and need. I asked our partner if he had anything we could give them. He said he had a case of corn meal in the back of his vehicle—and he willingly gave it to me.

We were able to give each family one five-pound bag. You would have thought it was Christmas morning. Everyone was smiling and laughing. They thanked me and some even hugged me. It left an indelible memory.

The African villagers told me their greatest need was water—they were dying. I had the opportunity to give words of encouragement and hope. But I knew I had to do more, so I asked our partner to drive me to the district governmental offices.

The officials described the crisis. They needed to drill wells immediately if they were going to save lives. I didn't even know what it cost to drill a well, but the words were out of my mouth: "We will do it. Somehow, we will do it!"

When I returned home, I shared the need and my experiences. I challenged everyone I knew to do something bigger than themselves—to make a difference in someone else's life, to be moved with compassion. I wasn't prepared for their response. The money for the wells was raised in one week, and the life-giving water soon began to flow.

Since that day, we have been providing clean water in countries all over the world. Hundreds of thousands of lives have been saved through having their most basic need, clean water, met with compassion and hope. But so much more needs to be done. Children are still suffering needlessly from a lack of clean water.

There are two purposes for writing this book. The first is to raise awareness and the second is to invite others to join the cause . . . **the cause of bringing clean water to millions.**

I have co-authored this book with my daughter Noel Brewer Yeatts, who shares my passion and vision to provide children with clean water. As World Help's vice president, she has worked closely with children for many years. Traveling to the corners of the world, she has hugged them, listened to them, and reached out to help.

Because this account is a combination of our research, experiences, and opinions, we have written the book using one voice. The first person storytelling style is from our combined points of view.

Some of the names and details have been altered to protect the identity of the children and their privacy.

Within the following pages, we have shared the compelling statistics and stories to help the children whose lives have been impacted through a lack of clean water. We have done our best to provide the most up-to-date information, but many statistics are constantly changing.

Thank you to our amazing writing and editing team, Nancy, Kim, Shelly, Sally, Christa, and Justin, and to my assistant DC Bowden who is also a professional photographer. Thank you for capturing the incredible images in this book. To Mark Brewer, a creative genius who is passionate about this cause. And finally to my wife Patty, Noel's mother, thank you for 38 years of dreaming the dream with me.

It is our sincere hope that with this glimpse into the lives of children who have no access to clean water, you will be touched.

And in turn, you will join the cause . . .

. . . cause**life**

. . . water equals life

Vernon Brewer

children

Six thousand children died today from water-related illnesses.[7]

—UNICEF

children

It is hot.

Even for Africa it is hot today. And it is only morning.

Fortunately for young Bashira, there is shade under her favorite mango tree. Ever since she can remember, the tree's spreading branches have been her escape from the sun.

The mango tree lies at the edge of her village so she can clearly see the collection of small huts. The village is of average size for Africa with just over 200 families. In all, there are nearly 1,000 villagers.[8] The huts look almost exactly alike. They are round with walls made of mud and manure mixed with straw. The roofs look like flattened cones and are made out of different branches and reeds that have dried to a pale yellow.

It's not long before her mother calls out, "Majee. Majee!" It's the Swahili word for water and this call is meant for Bashira. Her mother is standing in front of their hut waving two, five-gallon, yellow containers. In Africa, these are called jerry cans.

So begins a normal day for the 13-year-old. In the morning, she is sent by her mother to fetch water for the family. Bashira doesn't know the concept of running water, unless it's running in a creek or a river. The idea of a faucet is foreign, and she has never seen a toilet that flushes. Only half of the village has access to a latrine. The other half simply uses the fields or anywhere else that is convenient.[9]

Bashira is one of the 1.1 billion people in the world who does not have access to improved water sources.[10] This means a long walk every day for her family's water. And when she finally gets there, the water will be completely contaminated.

She has older brothers that could help with this chore, but they will be in school. For the most part, fetching water is left to women and girls in Uganda, as it is in most developing countries. This keeps the vast majority of girls out of school. Of the 121 million children worldwide who are not receiving any education, the majority are girls.[11]

Bashira also had two younger brothers. They used to help, but both fell ill and died. Diseases from unsafe water

over 1 billion people in the world have no access to improved water sources.

and poor sanitation are responsible for half the deaths in children under 5 in Uganda. In fact, over 2 million unsafe drinking water deaths occur in the world each year and the majority are children.[12]

Many other children across her village have perished from unclean water and the diseases it brings. For Bashira, early death is a part of life from which there is no escape.

To collect the water, Bashira must walk almost four miles just to reach the source. This is the average distance women in Africa and Asia must walk every day to get water.[13] But there are those who walk farther than that. When she doesn't feel like making the trek, Bashira's mother chides her with a reminder that some women and children walk nearly twice the distance.

She leaves early in the morning because arriving late at the water source could mean a long wait in line. That can add hours to the return trip, getting her back home late in the afternoon. Some girls in the village leave at three every morning so they will have enough time for their other chores.

Bashira makes her way along the narrow roads and winding paths as familiar to her as her own village. She knows each step by heart, and over the course of the two-hour walk, she sings her favorite songs in her native Swahili to pass the time.

Finally, she can see the glint of the sun off the greenish-brown water. This is the water source, a small pond and a feeble creek that feeds it. The water is dirty and the edges of the pond are covered with a green scum and animal waste. Two cows cool themselves off by wading up to their necks in the middle of the pond.

There is a throng of women and children, and the sound

over 2 million unsafe drinking water deaths occur in the world each year and the majority are children.

of buckets plunking down into the water fills the air. This is not only the water source for her village but for many other villages in the surrounding area. The smaller children are half-dressed, while others are wearing mostly rags. Many are not wearing shoes.

Three-quarters of the pond's edges are inaccessible by the overgrown shrubs and thorns. Bashira knows better than to even attempt walking over to the other side. Snakes, scorpions, and predatory animals need water too, and she must keep a careful eye where she steps. She also tries to stay out of the water. The last time she waded in, she came out with a large leech on her leg. Even in the middle of the day the mosquitoes are out in force as tiny swarms hovering over the pond incessantly bite her. During the rainy season, people in some areas of Africa can receive up to 100 infectious mosquito bites per month.[14]

Bashira waits in line for over an hour, talking to the other girls while she waits. Finally, after filling her two containers weighing 40 pounds each, she will carry them four miles back to her mother. The return trip always takes much longer. No matter how many times she carries water, her shoulders always burn and the young girl has to rest several times before reaching home.

Hours later, arriving back in the village, her two older brothers are returning from school. Bashira follows them into her family's hut and sets the cans on the dirt floor. Her mother takes one can and pours some into a pot for cooking. She puts cassava root, a carbohydrate staple in much of Africa, in to boil for dinner.

Her mother then pours some water in a small basin to use for washing the dishes when they are done eating. The other can is set aside and will be used for hand washing and bathing.

The family has never seen bacteria, read about it, or even been told it exists. They have no way of knowing that in some areas of Uganda, 90 percent of all water samples taken contained E. Coli.[15] They don't understand that the diarrhea that causes dehydration and death comes from the water they drink every day.

Bashira helps her mother with different chores until time to help prepare dinner. Afterwards there are few reasons to stay up, especially since they do not have electricity. Bashira cannot read or write, since she doesn't have time for both school and collecting water. When it grows dark, she puts a mat on the dirt floor, lies down, and falls asleep.

This is Bashira's day. Very little of it changes. When the sun rises tomorrow, she will once again walk for water, wait in line, and make the long trek back to her small hut.

She does not pursue any ambitions. Her dreams stop at the village's edge.

Ambitions and dreams do not have a place in a life where every day the biggest question is survival. Each day brings another battle to find water, food, and to not get sick. Her whole life is funneled down to meeting the most important need she has every day—self-preservation. Survival is her only goal.

namazzi

The next morning, in a different village in rural Uganda, 10-year-old Namazzi wakes up. The early morning sun

> during the rainy season, people in some areas of africa can receive up to 100 infectious mosquito bites per month.

pierces through the holes in her mud hut and stirs everyone inside.

It's crowded as her two brothers and younger sister also awaken and begin their day. Her mother is outside starting breakfast. Namazzi can smell the familiar scent of eggs and cassava root. She must help her sister get ready and then help her mother prepare breakfast.

Just like Bashira, Namazzi must also walk to collect water. She picks up two jerry cans and starts down the center path through her village. The roosters and hens scatter in front of her and the familiar sound of bleating goats fills the air. She can almost taste the warm goat's milk she will get with breakfast.

Her village is slightly larger than Bashira's, and it takes her only a few minutes to reach the outskirts. But for

Namazzi, this is as far as she will have to walk. Ten minutes and she's at her village's water source.

Her young friends are already beginning to gather here. They create a small, energetic crowd rippling with laughter and smiles. This is one of Namazzi's favorite times of the day, even if it is a chore. All her friends are here and the fun is contagious.

She makes her way through the group and up to a small five-by-five concrete platform, placing her water cans down with the others that have been gathered under a large metal spout. Three boys have already piled onto the long handle on the other end of the spout and begin the up-and-down movement of the pump.

There is nothing for a moment except for the squeak of the handle . . .

Then sputtering . . .

Then with another pump . . . clear, clean water pours from the well.

cause**life**

The younger children squeal with joy. This is still so new and exciting for them. It's something unbelievable, something they could never have imagined.

As Namazzi watches the water flow, she thinks back to when the well was first installed. Strangers came to her village. The villagers had not been sure of them and the large trucks they brought. Their equipment was noisy and it scared her. Most of the village didn't really accept or trust the men.

Once the well was drilled, she did not like the taste of the water. To her it tasted like salt. Why drink salty water that tastes funny instead of the water she had been drinking?

So even after the well was finished, it sat there gathering dust. Namazzi would walk right past it to the small creek that was her normal water source.

But the men who put in the well kept coming back. One man in particular was Ugandan and he would gather the villagers around him. He told them in their own language that they should drink this water. He said it was "clean."

in some areas of uganda, 90 percent of all water samples taken contained e. coli.

He told Namazzi and her village that the water they had been drinking was making them sick and causing many of the children to die. The man said if they drank the new water, even if it tasted funny to them, they would be healthy and fewer of their children would die. He told them to use it to grow vegetables and fruits and to let their animals drink this water so they would not have parasites.

This was all new to Namazzi. But since they started drinking the clean water, there really was a difference. In fact, most of the children in the village were getting healthier.

Although she didn't understand the science behind it, wonderful things were happening. Since she and her friends were drinking the amount of clean water they needed, their bodies were able to absorb the nutrients from food, helping to alleviate malnutrition.

And because she no longer had to spend her days hauling water, Namazzi even had time to go to school with her brothers and sister where she was learning to read and write. On average, the clean water, combined with improved sanitation and hand washing, dropped the village cases of diarrhea by 95 percent.

Now as she watches the sparkling water overflow the containers, she is thankful beyond words for the well and how her village has changed.

Each day is now different for Namazzi. When she wakes up, survival is not a question; it's a fact. Because of clean water there is better food. Because of the better food and overall health, there is increased production in the village. And school for Namazzi is no longer just a dream.

water as a seed

Bashira and Namazzi lead two very different lives. From the surface, it may be difficult to pinpoint what makes those differences, but they all come from the same root . . . water.

In this sense, we can think of water as a seed.

From the seed of contaminated water grows a tree, and every branch on it has a resulting bad condition. Low on the tree would be a branch of waterborne parasites and another one of bacteria. Other branches would bear typhoid, dysentery, malaria, and cholera. Still branching out higher would be malnutrition.

You might be surprised to find that one branch is a lack of education. Children cannot go to school because their parents need them to help the family survive. Walking for water is the most common chore that keeps children busy during the day. They can survive without an education, but they cannot survive without water. Also, drinking a steady supply of contaminated water makes children sick, if not dying. Sick children do not go to school.

This tree would contain branch after branch of horrible conditions that cause sickness, contributing to a life of illiteracy, poverty, and preventable death.

Short-term solutions such as trucking in water or food are

just that, short term. These quick fixes absolutely save lives, but they do not create self-sustainability. Instead, they create dependence without progress.

The root problem will still be dirty water. That root must be ripped from the ground and in its place planted the seed of clean water.

The tree that grows from the seed of clean water is strong and healthy, vibrant and full of life. Its branches spread far and wide. These are the branches of health, nourishment, and progress.

High mortality rates drop because babies no longer suffer from parasites and diarrhea. There is more food from gardens and irrigated land. Families eat what they need and have some leftover to sell at the market.

Children can do their chores, help out their families, and still have time for school. Some may eventually attend a university where they will receive a higher education, bringing hope to their villages and communities.

Two different children. They live in the same country. They speak the same language. Water is the common factor and water also makes the difference.

Water changes children.

health

"We shall not finally defeat AIDS, tuberculosis, malaria, or any of the other infectious diseases that plague the developing world until we have also won the battle for safe drinking water, sanitation and basic health care."[16]

—Kofi Annan, former United Nations
  Secretary General

health

Dilapidated shacks jut from the barren Guatemalan hillside. Brightly colored clothing hangs on lines and contrasts against the brownness of the landscape and makeshift shelters. It is strangely quiet for the middle of the day.

This village is known as Limones. Translated, it means Limes. But there are no green limes to be seen at all. In fact, there are no red tomatoes, yellow corn, green lettuce, or even the pale pink of drying beans. Brown is all there is.

If you were to spend time in this village, you would soon discover there is no electricity. There is no running water.

The water is there, but it is hidden in a place you might not want to see. At the bottom of the hill, down a narrow trail and steep incline, is a small creek. Although, creek may not be the best word for it. At one point it might have flowed and maybe it will again in the rainy season, but for now it just sits. It is stagnant and covered in a green scum. When you get close, you can smell a foul odor that makes you sick.

What is seriously depressing is it only takes a few minutes of waiting to see a couple of young children and a mother walking down to the water. Each child has a small pail or plastic container. And sure enough, they wade into the filthy water and begin gathering their supply for the day.

In the village of Limones, every single child drinks this water.

And every single child is sick.

It is estimated that "86 percent of all urban wastewater in Latin America . . . is discharged untreated into rivers, lakes, and oceans."[17] This is one of the reasons why there are thousands of villages in Guatemala like Limones, and thousands more children are dying because of it. Contaminated water is bringing disease and death.

Unclean water, together with the poor sanitation it creates, is the number one killer in the entire world.[18] Combine war, malaria, HIV/AIDS, and even traffic accidents . . . Dirty water still kills more people.[19]

antonia

Antonia lives in an area of Guatemala known as Chiquimula. I'm told it has the highest rate of infant mortality in all of Guatemala. There are over 300 families in her village and each one is struggling to survive.

Our Guatemalan partner is a regular fixture there. Through our help, he is able to take them food and medicine. However, this village still needs clean water.

He has rescued many children from Chiquimula who have been close to death. In fact, he rescues thousands of children from the remotest parts of Guatemala and brings them to his Baby Rescue Center. Here, children receive medical care, food, clean water, and love.

His greatest struggle is not in saving them, but in keeping the ones he has saved healthy. He knows some of the children he returns will become sick and once again need rescuing.

Little Antonia had a brother, but our partner could not save him in time. However, he was able to rescue Antonia's sister. She underwent an amazing recovery at the center and, when better, was taken back to her parents.

At the time, Antonia wasn't sick, but within a few months she needed urgent medical care herself. When our partner went back to the village to rescue her, he found Antonia's sister had become ill again and recently died.

Although Antonia is now healthy, our partner fears that without the clean water she needs, he will be returning to rescue her time and time again.

If you asked why these children keep getting sick, he would say just one word, "Water." They have food, medicine, clothing, and shelter. The only thing they don't have is clean water, and it's killing them!

> unclean water, together with the poor sanitation it creates, is the number one killer in the entire world. combine war, malaria, hiv/aids, and even traffic accidents ... dirty water still kills more people.

A single sip of water is all it takes to be infected. A single drop of water can contain over 1 billion bacterial organisms.[20] The following is only a partial list of water-related diseases:

Diarrhea

- Each year there are more than 4 billion cases of diarrhea, which causes 2.2 million deaths.[21] Five thousand children will die today from diarrhea.[22] One of the effects of diarrhea is dehydration. When a child begins to suffer dehydration, the only choice for them is more dirty water. This is a death sentence for millions of children.

- One very important aspect of diarrhea is the direct link to malnutrition. Diarrhea causes food to not be properly digested and stored by the body.[23] Even if it does not result in death, it can lead to "stunting of growth, intellectual impairment, and diminished productive and creative capacities."[24]

Malaria

- "Forty-one percent of the world's population

lives in areas where malaria is transmitted."[25] Of this percentage, 1.3 million die of malaria and 90 percent of them are young children.[26] Transmission rates are dramatically increased due to unmanaged water sources.

Trachoma

- An unbelievable 500 million people are at risk for this disease that leads to blindness.[27] And 128 million children are affected.[28] There is a strong correlation between trachoma and a lack of face washing, most often due to the absence of near-by clean water sources.[29] The vast majority of these cases lie in sub-Saharan Africa. In Uganda, close to 40 percent of all children are affected by trachoma.[30]

Worms and Parasites

- Simply being infected by worms and parasites can lead to cognitive impairment, massive dysentery, or anemia.[31] These are conditions a child may not die from, but severely lessen their opportunity to attend school. Digestion and the absorption of food are also affected by worms, causing bloated stomachs, pain, and diarrhea in children.[32]

Typhoid

- Typhoid fever is the result of bacteria ingested by eating contaminated foods and, most commonly, drinking unclean water. According to the World Health Organization, there are as many as 21 million cases and 600,000 deaths from typhoid fever annually.[33] In some countries, 90 percent of typhoid cases are children ages 5-19.[34]

Cholera

- The World Health Organization reports that "Cholera is a substantial health burden in many countries in Africa, Asia, and South and Central America, where it is endemic." Cholera is an intestinal infection received through contaminated water, as well as food. Ninety-four percent of all reported cases occur in Africa. It is estimated that 120,000 people die each year from cholera. In addition, 3-5 million new cases of cholera are reported worldwide annually.[35] Even if water is trucked in during an outbreak, it is often not enough.[36]

"About 29,000 children under the age of 5—21 each minute—die every day, mainly from preventable causes," reports UNICEF. "An Ethiopian child is 30 times more likely to die by his or her fifth birthday than a child in Western Europe … Malnutrition and the lack of safe water and sanitation contribute to half of all these children's deaths."[37]

Living in a developed country can make us forget that the majority of the world's population deals with these diseases every day. Most of us rarely, if ever, think about some horrible life-threatening disease that might make its way into our glass.

The only times we hear the words, "Don't drink the water!" are usually in travel warnings to countries in Latin America, Asia, and Africa. Yet, children living in those countries drink the water every day … and they are not okay. Their bodies are not used to the bacteria. They are dying from it.

> a single sip of water is all it takes to be infected. a single drop of water can contain over 1 billion bacterial organisms.

One of our Villages of Hope lies outside Kampala, the capital of Uganda. We provided this village for over 900 orphaned and disadvantaged children. These children come from devastating poverty and from slums where they played in streams filled with raw sewage. But here they find peace and safety. They receive clean water, nutritious food, clothing, and an education.

However, the nearest village is still a very dangerous place for children. According to our partner, 70 percent of all infants born in that village die due to dirty water and the resulting diseases. Typhoid and malaria are the major killers.

These diseases are treatable, and parents can see the tell-tale warning signs enough to know their child needs medical aid. But in developing countries, a car is a luxury and hospitals are few and far between. Many children die before they can reach help.

medicine is not the solution

Medicine saves lives and there needs to be more access to medicine for those in poverty-stricken countries. But in the end, medicine is only part of the solution. It is only a bandage on a cancer. The ultimate solution and cure is clean water.

What many do not realize is that without clean water, some medications children receive are not as effective as they should be. And in some cases, they can even be harmful.

An example of this is the distribution of antiretroviral drugs in developing countries. Known as ARVs, these drugs are used to treat HIV/AIDS and have improved and saved countless lives. But the lack of water and the resulting aggravation of malnutrition and famine can cause these medications to be harmful and painful.

The ARVs must be taken for life, without interruptions. They are extremely powerful and when taken without food and clean water, severe reactions can occur. When this happens in an infected child or adult, the medication is almost always stopped. This is not only from the painful reaction, but also through a misunderstanding of how the drugs work. The HIV/AIDS virus then becomes stronger and can mutate and eventually become resistant to any medication.

Even when there is food and water, there is often not enough. One mother explained her dilemma. "Some of us hardly get food to eat as our husbands are already dead, leaving behind the children. We, the HIV-positive mothers, are the ones taking care of the rest of the family. We prefer to let the children get the food, as they cannot fend for themselves."[38]

joan

Joan is a 12-year-old girl living in Uganda. Her home is a three-room hut made of mud bricks and dirt floors. Joan's street is an uneven dirt path barely passable with a four-wheel drive vehicle. Her water faucet is a well that lies miles away.

All of these difficulties pale in comparison to the fact that Joan is dying of HIV/AIDS.

cause**life**

> about 29,000 children under the age of
> 5—21 each minute—die every day, main-
> ly from preventable causes.

Joan is part of an entire family devastated by this disease. Her father died from AIDS, leaving his wife Ruth and their seven children completely helpless. The stigma of HIV/AIDS has kept other villagers away and the family isolated from local help.

After her husband died, Ruth was advised to take a blood test. She took Joan with her, who had a severe, nagging sickness. As an added measure, Ruth also brought her youngest child Michael, who was only a few months old.

As the nurse gave her the test results, all Ruth could hear were the words ringing in her ears over and over again . . . "Positive."

Ruth: positive for HIV/AIDS.
Joan: positive for HIV/AIDS.
Michael: positive for HIV/AIDS.

Every case was terminal; it was only a matter of time.

So in a small corner of the world, a family began their struggle to survive against incredible odds. With no money for antiretroviral medications, inadequate food and water, no schooling or even clothing, their hope slowly melted away in the stifling African heat.

Joan quietly went about her daily chores . . . fetching water, helping her mother care for Michael, cooking, and gathering fruit from the meager papaya trees in their yard.

Then one day a man came to Joan's home. He was warm, compassionate, and he greeted them with a huge smile that seemed to proclaim hope. He didn't shrink in fear as others did. Instead he reached out and hugged them. That man was one of our Ugandan partners and he was going to help change their lives.

A well was provided in their village and clean water and food began to be delivered to their home. They finally had bread, eggs, rice, salt, meat, and vegetables. This was the nutrition Joan and her family would need for the antiretrovirals. Joan also started receiving soap, toothbrushes, extra clothes, and many other items that for so long she had gone without.

Through our Child Sponsorship Program, Joan was able to attend school. In fact, five of her siblings, old enough for school, were enrolled as well. She received a new school uniform made of bright red African cloth and shiny new black shoes.

Ruth, Joan, and her infant brother also began to receive antiretroviral medications. Their health immediately improved and kept the disease from progressing as quickly.

These acts of compassion opened a door through which Jesus could be shared. Joan and the rest of her family soon became Christ followers.

On a recent visit to Uganda, Ruth and Joan expressed their gratitude. Standing in front of their home, Ruth held Joan close to her side. As tears streamed from her eyes, Ruth said, "Thank you. Without your help, I would be dead."

There are millions of children like Joan and they all need our help. They all need clean water to transform their health and their future.

It is often said that the best way to treat an illness is to make sure you don't get it in the first place. Although it almost seems too simple, the best medicine really is prevention.

Prevention doesn't have to be bottles of supplements, exercise programs, and a low-cholesterol diet.

Prevention can be as simple as a cup of clean water.

Water changes health.

poverty

"Without adequate clean water, there can be no escape from poverty."[39]

—Klaus Töpfer, former Director of the United Nations Environment Program

poverty

"I grew up in a place where it is not shocking to hear about someone who got killed or hijacked, because it really makes no difference," he said. "I grew up with not just the challenge of living life the way it should be lived, with love and sharing amongst the people, but I grew up with the challenge of having to grow without the guidance of my parents.

"Like many ordinary South Africans, I grew up in the shacks of Cape Town, a place where poor people do bad things to other people to make a living. It is a place where no one wants to live because you see danger everywhere."

Sitting across from me was a grown man. But as I watched Thando share his story, I could see the reflection of a frightened little boy in his eyes. Like so many children in the sub-Saharan region of Africa, he grew up under the heavy burden of poverty. Poverty creates a fertile breeding ground for diseases, contributing to hopelessness and desperation.

As I talked with him, I could sense he only wanted to focus on the future. The past was too painful. I carefully asked several questions trying to understand his story.

But he answered each one with a positive response. It was only later that Thando was able to communicate his troubled past.

"My people living in these places, called shacks or squatter camps, are living in poverty. They are always the ones that are abused the most. They suffer the most."

As an orphan, his life was not easy. "No one else was going to provide for me. I had to keep focused," he said. Thando, along with other orphans and destitute families, were crowded together in slums of makeshift housing. In these shacks, he lived in squalor and filth. No running water and poor sanitation left many ill. The stench was unbearable and food was scarce. Thando had to beg for barely enough to live. In addition to his daily struggle for survival, he also had to deal with the emotional and physical scars of a terrifying accident.

"The shack I was staying in caught on fire and burned to the ground. A baby that was with me in the house died, but I came out alive." The day I met Thando, I noticed he still carries the scars on his face and hands from the fire. The scars of poverty will forever remain with him.

Worldwide, one out of every two children lives in the most desperate poverty conditions.[40]

How do you define poverty?

We tend to define poverty by things we want, not by things we truly need to survive. We feel "poor" when we cannot afford everything we desire.[41]

The vast majority of those classified as poor in America own their own homes according to the Census Bureau. They also own their own car, have a VCR or DVD player, and own one or two color televisions. By the rest of the world's standards, this would be considered quite comfortable living.[42]

The poor always endure hardship and pain regardless of their level of poverty or where they live. But all poverty is not the same.

> worldwide, one out of every two children lives in the most desperate poverty conditions.

The 1.4 billion people living in extreme poverty are not just poor.[43] They would be described as living in "absolute" poverty. The United Nations has defined absolute poverty as "a condition characterized by severe deprivation of human needs, including food, safe drinking water, sanitation facilities, health, shelter, education, and information."[44]

Poverty means loss of freedom, loss of dignity, and loss of control over the fundamental course of your life.

A Jamaican woman described poverty this way, "Poverty is like living in a jail, living under bondage, waiting to be free."[45]

The grip of poverty on developing countries is choking the life out of many children and their families. These are desperate people without choices. Most of us have no idea about the harsh reality of life for the children of poverty as shown in the following report:

> *The physical health needs of children and youth are closely related to the broader problems of poverty. The staggering reality is that more than 1 billion of*

the world's children—56 percent—are living in poverty or severe deprivation! A stunning 37 percent of the world's children, more than 674 million, live in absolute poverty.

Additionally, children living in what is defined as "severe deprivation" struggle with a "lack of income and productive resources to ensure sustainable livelihoods." . . . They are also victims of "hunger and malnutrition, ill health, limited access or lack of access to education and other basic services, increased morbidity and mortality from illness, homelessness, and inadequate housing, unsafe environments, social discrimination, and exclusion." . . .

- *Over one-third of children have to live in dwellings with more than five people per room*
- *134 million children have no access to any school whatsoever*
- *Over half a billion children have no toilet facilities whatsoever*
- *Almost half a billion children lack access to published information of any kind[46]*

> the staggering reality is that more than
> 1 billion of the world's children—56 per-
> cent—are living in poverty or severe de-
> privation!

Mother Teresa taught us, "In the poor we meet Jesus in His most distressing disguises."[47] Throughout the Bible, over 3,000 verses have been found that reference the idea of the poor and alleviating poverty.[48]

Early Christians said that if a child starves to death while a Christian has extra food, then that person is guilty of murder. One of the fathers of the Church, Basil the Great, wrote in the fourth century: "When someone strips a man of his clothes, we call him a thief. And one who might clothe the naked and does not—should not he be given the same name? The bread in your cupboard belongs to the hungry; the coat in your wardrobe belongs to the naked, the shoes you let rot belong to the barefoot; the money in your vaults belong to the destitute."[49]

But can we really end poverty? Should we even try?

give them a chance

In *The Life You Can Save*, Peter Singer describes what he calls "futility thinking." If we are not careful, too often we start to believe "that aid to the poor is 'drops in the ocean,' implying that it is not worth giving, because no matter how much we do, the ocean of people in need will seem just as vast as it was before."[50]

While we find it hard to understand the lives of children in poverty, we also miss one of the greatest causes of poverty around the world—the lack of clean water.

For the poor, they are caught in a no-win situation and a deadly cycle. Their poverty prevents them from access to clean water. And their lack of clean water almost always ensures they will never escape the death grip of poverty.

a stunning 37 percent of the world's children, more than 674 million, live in absolute poverty.

The World Bank reports, "Water is crucial to human life in a countless number of ways. It is important not only for the everyday needs of drinking, washing, and cleaning, but also for growing crops to feed the population, for generating power to provide electricity, and for maintaining ecosystems such as wetlands. Overall, it plays a vital role in people's livelihoods, the growth of the economy, and the sustenance and health of all species."[51]

It is estimated that nearly 5 percent of the Gross Domestic Product (GDP) is lost in African countries due to the sickness and disease caused by unclean water.[52]

The absence of an adequate supply of water makes it nearly impossible to grow crops which provide income to families and communities. Without clean water, people are sick and can't work or attend school. And, without clean, safe water, poverty never goes away.

At the 2000 UN Millennium Summit, 189 nations and many other international organizations agreed on eight strategic goals (Millennium Development Goals) that would reduce extreme poverty by 2015:

it is estimated that nearly 5 percent of the gross domestic product (gdp) is lost in african countries due to the sickness and disease caused by unclean water.

- Eradicate Extreme Hunger and Poverty
- Achieve Universal Primary Education
- Promote Gender Equality and Empower Women
- Reduce Child Mortality
- Improve Maternal Health
- Combat HIV/AIDS, Malaria, and Other Diseases
- Ensure Environmental Sustainability
- Develop a Global Partnership for Development[53]

A crucial part of their plan is to cut in half the number of people who lack access to clean and safe water.[54]

Our world leaders even know that one of the best ways to help end poverty is by providing clean water. But despite their power and influence, they will never reach their goals alone. We must all buy into this and we are all part of the solution.

> "if I look at the mass I will never act. if I look at the one, I will." —mother teresa

jefferson

In the hills of Guatemala, a 9-year-old boy named Jefferson dreams of one day becoming an architect and designing strong, magnificent buildings. But he and his four brothers and sisters are children of poverty.

Like so many others in his country, they live below the poverty line without access to clean water and other necessary resources.

Most people would say that Jefferson has very little chance of realizing his dreams.

But, he doesn't need much to make his dreams come true. He just needs a chance to escape the cycle of poverty his family has lived in for years and years.

It has been said, "Poverty is about hopes, dreams and how many people are prevented from dreaming."[55]

I don't want Jefferson to ever stop dreaming.

"If I look at the mass I will never act. If I look at the one, I will."[56] Mother Teresa said these words, and I can't imagine anyone else better understanding the masses of people in need.

The concept of poverty can be overwhelming, and the thought of making a difference can seem daunting. So, we must narrow our focus.

Instead of picturing a "vast ocean of people," we must begin to see the one hurting child simply asking for clean water.

It all starts with one child, one well, and one person willing to make a difference.

Water changes poverty.

above

"The main cause of malnutrition . . . is not really lack of food, but the availability and accessibility of clean water." —Philippe Guyon Le Bouffi

above

Patty Brewer caring for children at the Baby Rescue Center in Guatemala.

right

A cascade of hands enjoys the clean water that now flows from a newly drilled well.

below

Our *Christmas for an Orphan* program gives children the opportunity to celebrate Christmas year-round as they receive basic necessities and a few fun items they would not otherwise have.

right

Vernon Brewer oversees a well being drilled in the village of Pueblo Modelo in Guatemala.

below

Tom Thompson and Tony Foglio deliver sewing machines to vocational school graduates in Gulu, Uganda.

above

Orphaned and needy children are receiving food, clothing, an education, and clean drinking water at Villages of Hope throughout Africa.

above
Our partners in Guatemala are feeding 150,000 needy children and families every day.

right
In Africa and Asia, children and women walk an average of four miles to reach a water source.

below

Katwe is one of the worst slums in Uganda. Raw sewage runs through
the center of the slum, contaminating the water, children, livestock, and
ground.

right

Vernon and his daughter, Noel Brewer Yeatts, visit an AIDS ravaged village in South Africa.

below

"Frisby" Davidson hands out *Christmas for an Orphan* boxes to children in Guatemala.

above

According to UNICEF, unclean water is the number one killer in the entire world. Combine war, malaria, HIV/AIDS, and even traffic accidents . . . Dirty water still kills more people.

above

Even the youngest children must walk long distances to gather their family's water.

right

The look of joy in this boy's face is unmistakable. He has hope and a future through a clean water well.

below

Two girls enjoy the clean water that is now available right next to their home in Guatemala.

right

Annually, clean water could prevent 860,000 child deaths from malnutrition.

below

DC Bowden visits with Joan in Uganda.

above

Skip Taylor loads 50-pound bags of food on mules to be delivered high in the Guatemalan mountains.

above

"Education is the most powerful weapon which you can use to change the world."
—Nelson Mandela

right

Knowledge of basic sanitation is very poor in developing countries. In Rwanda, this woman cleans her water containers with dirt, straw, and contaminated water.

Riaz Chauthani and Robbie Lee dedicate a clean water well they provided for a rural Guatemalan village.

right

Each year in Africa, 40 billion working hours are spent just on fetching water.

below

A single drop of water can contain over one billion bacterial organisms. And it only takes one single sip to become infected.

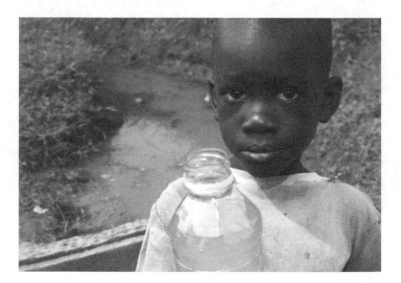

above

Paul Ehlke dedicates a well he provided in the village of El Rincon de los Limones in Guatemala.

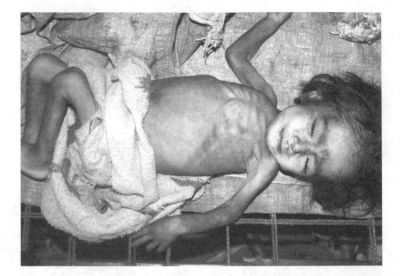

above

Antonia was dying when she was rescued by our Guatemalan partner and brought to the Baby Rescue Center.

right

This is Antonia after only a few months of receiving the help she needed at the center.

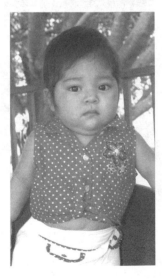

below

Children in El Rincon de los Limones play under the new clean water well.

right

Mark Brewer helps pump a clean water well in Rwanda.

below

Dedication of a new Village of Hope in Uganda, for children who are HIV/AIDS victims.

above

Clean water can provide children a healthy life full of opportunity.

above

Noel spends time with children at a village of grass huts near Lusaka, Zambia.

right

Sandy Sansing talks with Ugandan children.

below

"About 29,000 children under the age of five—21 every minute—die each
day, mainly from preventable causes." —UNICEF

right

The gift of clean water is not temporary, it is the gift of life that lasts for a lifetime.

below

Medicine is critical, but unless children have clean water to drink, it can lose its effectiveness.

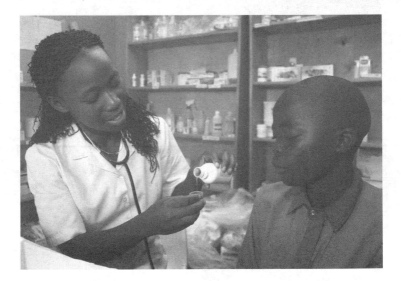

above

Children drink clean water from a well in Rwanda.

above

Globally, children lose 443 million school days each year because of waterborne illnesses.

below

Tom Thompson, Sandy Sansing, Vernon Brewer, and Alex Mitala stand in front of the Luttisi Medical Clinic provided by Sandy. It is the only medical clinic in this entire rural area of Uganda.

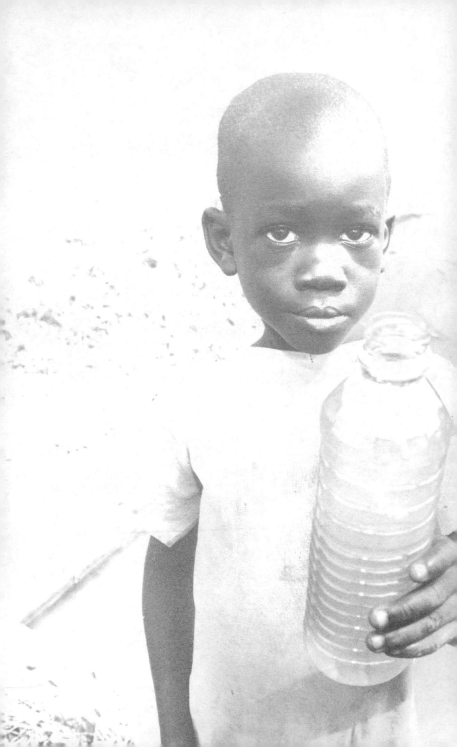

hunger

"The main cause of malnutrition . . . is not really lack of food, but the availability and accessibility of clean water."[57]

—Philippe Guyon Le Bouffi, former head of the United Nations World Food Program in Chad

hunger

She stands there, tiny and helpless. Her eyes are dark and have a hopeless stare to them. Her belly is distended, her chest is collapsed, and her face is lean and gaunt. She can't keep the flies off her.

We have all seen an image like that. We know the look of hunger, even though we try to look away at times. Something pulls at our hearts and we think, "If only . . . if only I was there and could give her something to eat. She is starving and a single piece of bread or a slice of fruit could make a difference."

In these situations, what we see is a hungry, malnourished child. While food is critical if they are to survive, the first course of treatment is usually rehydration with clean water.

When we see the gruesome effects of malnutrition, we tend to automatically think it is only the result of a lack of food. It is not so much a lack of food, but a lack of nutrients. The life-giving nutrients are not being absorbed due to the different diseases and parasites brought about by contaminated water.

we know the look of hunger, even though we try to look away at times.

In Guatemala, 44 percent of children suffer from chronic malnutrition. But it is the lack of clean water that is the main factor for this high number.[58]   Every year 860,000 child deaths from malnutrition could be prevented by providing clean water.[59]

According to UNICEF, "Parasites, transferred by water-borne contamination, consume nutrients, aggravate malnutrition, retard children's physical development and result in poor school attendance and performance."[60]

In turn, these parasites from dirty water also cause one of the deadliest illnesses in the world, diarrhea. The loss of hydration has an immediate effect on the body. Nutrients are not absorbed and malnutrition takes hold.

In a final turn that completes this vicious cycle, malnutrition causes more diarrhea. It can also lead to a serious infection such as pneumonia. It is this cycle of dirty water and malnutrition that claims so many lives.

food wasn't enough

Our Guatemalan partner traveled many hours to arrive at the mountain village of Chastutu. He knew a child there was close to death. As he made his way through the village he heard a woman crying from inside one of the shacks. He knew he was too late. As he entered the home, the mother was holding her baby daughter's body with tears in her eyes. There was nothing he could do except offer to bury the baby for her mother. But she was not ready to give up her daughter yet. In the end, she held her baby for six hours. He was patient and when she was ready, he buried the baby and held a small service.

This baby girl had access to food, but she died of malnutrition. Very simply, food wasn't enough. Food wasn't enough when dirty water caused her to get trapped in a cycle of sickness that eventually claimed her life.

every year 860,000 child deaths from malnutrition could be prevented by providing clean water.

Billions of dollars are spent each year on providing food to under-developed countries. These shipments are vital to the lives of hundreds of millions of people. Yet, continuing to supply food does not completely address the true issue.

Food will not do a malnourished infant any good if his body cannot process it due to parasites and bacteria from contaminated water. This is evident when food production in developing countries is increased and malnutrition still devastates the population.[61]

What we must do is help provide clean water sources to those who are suffering.

no water . . . no crops

Crops are a common source of food and income for the poor. But just as common are failing crops, food shortages, and famine. Many of these crops fail to succeed because of either dirty water or lack of water altogether. Food production requires water:

Food	Water Needed to Produce (in Gallons)[62]
Glass of milk	52.83
Cup of coffee	36.98
Slice of bread	10.57
Egg	35.66
Apple	18.49
Hamburger	634

For even the most basic staples, large amounts of water are needed to sustain crops and livestock.

When dirty water is used to water the crops, it is loaded with human and animal feces and a myriad of parasites and bacteria. Water literally spreads disease and exposes even more people in the community to potential infection.

Along with the waterborne diseases, there is also a chemical threat. Developing countries heavily use powerful pesticides. Ninety-nine percent of all pesticide deaths in the world occur in these countries, although they account for only 25 percent of the total consumption.[63]

The rain washes the chemicals off the crops and down into the streams and ponds where they are consumed through drinking. If the chemicals stay on the food, they are commonly ingested due to a lack of food washing.

The malnutrition children are suffering from dramatically increases their body's sensitivity to pesticides and can accelerate their condition.

The only successful solution is irrigation with clean water. Irrigation is essential to increased food production. The 17 percent of land that is irrigated in the world is producing 40 percent of the global food supply.[64]

Irrigation also translates to an increase in a family's income. Through irrigation in Africa, the net income per family increases anywhere from $150 to $1,000.[65]

Just one small pump installed near a village well can irrigate over two acres of land with fresh, clean water. Several pumps can be used for even more irrigation.[66]

no water . . . no livestock

Besides crops, another staple for income and food is livestock.

"Nearly 2 billion people—a third of the world's population—derive at least some of their livelihood from farm animals, and nearly one person in eight depends almost entirely on livestock . . . livestock provide 20-60 percent of household income." For these people, livestock are the single most important investment they have.[67]

But it takes a large amount of water to keep livestock alive. If animals are exposed to contaminated water, they can become infected with worms and other parasites. If the animal is eaten, the worms are easily transmitted to humans.

These animals also contaminate water by becoming infected and then wading in the same source where it is collected for human consumption.

From waterborne diseases to crops and livestock, water is the common thread underlying many conditions that aggravate hunger and malnutrition in poverty-stricken countries.

Over 840 million people worldwide suffer from mal-nutrition. Seven hundred ninety-nine million of those live in developing countries and 153 million are young children.[68]

Our first thought will probably always be that we need to provide them with more food. Ending hunger will bring transformation, but providing food is not enough.

We must start with clean water, a single well in a village, an irrigation pump for crops. We can work on alleviating hunger through providing water.

over 840 million people worldwide suffer from malnutrition. seven hundred ninety-nine million of those live in developing countries and 153 million are young children.

If "a journey of a thousand miles begins with a single step," this transformation begins with a single drop.[69]

Water changes hunger.

education

"They talk about water in school. Water is precious . . . very precious."[70]

—Young boy from India

education

Can you remember the last time you thought of water as being precious? Was there ever a time you looked at it that way? Most of us simply take water for granted.

Benjamin Franklin once said, "When the well is dry, we learn the worth of water."[71] For millions of children around the world, they have already learned this difficult lesson. The question is, have we?

While the majority of the world struggles to find any kind of water source—clean or dirty—Americans alone spent about $16 billion last year on bottled water.[72] The United Nations estimates it would only "require an additional $30 billion a year to provide safe, clean drinking water to the entire planet." Globally, we spent three times that amount on bottled water in just one year.[73]

Meanwhile, a group of young girls are sitting in the hot African sun waiting. They have walked miles to the nearest water source they can find. Jugs in hand, they wait and wait and wait. The pipe the water trickles from is unpredictable. Sometimes the water comes, sometimes it does not. They can wait for hours. And sometimes, water may not flow for weeks.

> the united nations estimates it would only "require an additional $30 billion a year to provide safe, clean drinking water to the entire planet." globally, we spent three times that amount on bottled water in just one year.

After walking for hours and waiting for hours, the girls give out a sigh of relief when the water finally begins to slowly trickle out. But the excitement is only temporary. Tomorrow they will have to do the same thing over again . . . and every day after that.[74]

In Rwanda, children are walking one to three miles, carrying back 40 pounds of water four times a day. The constant need for water is time consuming and exhausting.

Around the world, 376 million children must walk more than 15 minutes to access water.[75] Studies show that in sub-Saharan Africa and many other areas around the world, women and young girls must walk an average of four miles every day just to provide water for their families.[76]

Each year in Africa, 40 billion working hours are spent just on fetching water.[77]

The consequences are tragic. Children have no time for school and the adults, especially the women, have little time left to pursue opportunities that would financially benefit their families. The long-term damage and ripple effects of this loss of time are too great to measure.

The world's poorest 1.4 billion people live on less than $1.25 a day.[78] These same people most likely lack a basic education. And it should be no surprise that a large part of this number—1.1 billion—lack access to clean water.[79]

Without access to clean water and without an education, the vicious cycle of poverty continues.

each year in africa, 40 billion working hours are spent just on fetching water.

In addition, communities without water do not thrive and there is usually no infrastructure for schools. Clean water provides small towns and villages with opportunities, an economy, a society, a culture, a life. Without water, communities literally dry up, and as always, it is the children who suffer the most.

Nabaru is a young boy from a small village outside Kampala, Uganda. He has not had a drop of clean water in his entire life. Not one drop. Every day he makes several trips to his only water source—a small dirty pond. There are no clean water wells nearby. Nabaru is 15 years old, but he cannot go to school because one does not exist in his village.

For the few lucky ones who have the opportunity to attend school in another village, their plans can be interrupted by sickness from water-related diseases. The end result is no education and no social development. Their young lives become destined to end the same place they started . . . deep in the heart of poverty.

Globally, children lose 443 million school days each year because of waterborne illnesses.[80]   And every year, 400 million children become infected with worms, which severely limits their learning potential.[81]

The bottom line is, when clean water is available, children are less likely to get sick and, therefore, they miss less school. In Malawi, strategic clean water improvements have raised school enrollment for girls to 94 percent.[82]

Stephanie Kinnunen of NEED Magazine reports, "Water is a necessity for all human beings, and clean drinking water is vital to maintain good health. The epicenters are a closer and cleaner source of water than most villages had previously. In addition, the time that is saved getting water each day, can now be spent on education or income-generating activities."[83]

globally, children lose 443 million school days each year because of waterborne illnesses. and every year, 400 million children become infected with worms, which severely limits their learning potential.

clean has a taste

Imagine drinking dirty water your whole life. It's bad for you, but you don't know it. There are billions of organisms swimming around in it determined to make you sick. But you have grown accustomed to the gritty and foul-smelling taste.

We think clean water would be immediately welcomed and gulped down from the first sight. But, unfortunately, many times, this is not the case.

In the village of Namayumba, Rwanda, stands a clean water well. Initially, the villagers would not drink from it. Instead, they walked an additional 300 yards to a filthy water source. The reason? They didn't like the salty taste of the clean water.

A boy named Habimana stood at another clean water well in Rwanda. However, instead of getting a drink there, he walked down to a dirty pond. When someone tried to tell him the water was not good, he simply shrugged his shoulders and said, "It's okay." He didn't understand the difference.

In addition to providing clean water, teachers are needed to educate people, especially the children, on the benefits of clean water, why it tastes different, and why they should still drink it.

second chances

By providing clean water, children will once again have a chance to attend school and receive an education that will be their first step toward a life of opportunity.

José was less than a year old when he was discovered sitting in a pool of mud in a remote village of Guatemala. His mother had left him outside in these terrible conditions for three days without food or water. José's mother was mentally unstable and had already caused his brother's death through neglect.

In addition, José was very sick. The dirty water and lack of food had caught up with this small infant.

Between the sickness and neglectful mother, José was destined to die before his first birthday. But God had

> in addition to providing clean water, teachers are needed to educate people, especially the children, on the benefits of clean water, why it tastes different, and why they should still drink it.

other plans for this special little boy. He was rescued by a kind man who provided him with medical care and slowly nursed him back to health.

José was given a second chance at life. He was given clean water, food, shelter, and lots of love. He was also given an education and a chance for a future.

Twenty years later, José is now attending a university.

His education is giving him knowledge and an incredible opportunity … a chance to give back. Every week José hikes up into the hills to rescue dying children. He sees himself in the face of every child he helps and knows what it will take to change their lives … clean water and an education.

> "education is the most powerful weapon which you can use to change the world."
> —nelson mandela

José knows that in order to keep the children from becoming ill, their families must have access to safe water. He knows that until the children stop getting sick, they will not be able to attend school. And until they can attend school, they will never have the opportunities they need to follow their dreams.

But while these children wait, José will continue to rescue as many children as he can find.

Nelson Mandela has said, "Education is the most powerful weapon which you can use to change the world."[84]

Water changes education.

you

"Thousands have lived without love, not one without water."[85]

—W.H. Auden, poet

you

On your way to work, you pass a small pond. On hot days, children sometimes play in the pond, which is only about knee-deep. The weather's cool today though, and the hour is early, so you are surprised to see a child splashing about in the pond. As you get closer, you see that it is a very young child, just a toddler, who is flailing about, unable to stay upright or walk out of the pond. You look for the parents or babysitter, but there is no one else around. The child is unable to keep his head above the water for more than a few seconds at a time. If you don't wade in and pull him out, he seems likely to drown. Wading in is easy and safe, but you will ruin the new shoes you bought only a few days ago, and get your suit wet and muddy. By the time you hand the child over to someone responsible for him, and change your clothes, you'll be late for work. What should you do? . . .

In 2007, something resembling this hypothetical situation actually occurred near Manchester, England. Jordon Lyon, a 10-year-old boy, leaped into a pond after his stepsister Bethany slipped in. He struggled to support her but went under himself. Anglers managed to pull Bethany out, but by then Jordon could no longer be seen. They raised the alarm, and two police community support officers soon arrived; they refused to enter the pond to find Jordon. He was later pulled out, but attempts at resuscitation failed. At the inquest on Jordon's death, the officers' inaction was defended on the grounds that they had not been trained to deal with such situations. The mother responded: 'If you're walking down the street and you see a child drowning you automatically go in that water... You don't have to be trained to jump in after a drowning child.[86]

This story presented in *The Life You Can Save* may seem extreme. But before you dismiss it, think about the meaning for one more minute. We would never imagine standing by as an innocent child drowns. But 6,000 children died today from water-related illnesses ... the equivalent of 20 jumbo jets crashing in one day.[87]

And we did very little to stop it.

Could it be that by not "jumping in," we are leaving children to drown? Are we leaving children thirsty and destined

six thousand children died today from water-related illnesses … the equivalent of 20 jumbo jets crashing in one day. and we did very little to stop it.

to die? Are these children we could have rescued?[88]

Bono, a rock star and leading activist, made it clear that we cannot ignore this problem when he said, "Future genera-tions … will know whether we answered the key question. The evidence will be the world around them. History will be our judge, but what's written is up to us. Who we are, who we've been, what we want to be remembered for. We can't say our generation didn't know how to do it. We can't say our generation couldn't afford to do it. And we can't say our generation didn't have reason to do it. It's up to us. We can choose to shift the responsibility, or … we can choose to shift the paradigm."[89]

change our perspective

The truth is, it is difficult for us to understand the global need for water. We walk to the faucet, turn the tap on, and the water flows. Most of us are always just steps away from fresh, cool, clean water. It is beyond our scope of reasoning and sensibility to consider walking miles upon miles to find a water source.

More water is used in one single flush of our toilets than the average person in Africa has for an entire day's intake, as well as household chores.[90]

As I write this chapter, I am looking out onto a big beautiful lake. Summer is almost here. Boats are buzzing

> "we can't say our generation didn't know how to do it. we can't say our generation couldn't afford to do it. and we can't say our generation didn't have reason to do it. it's up to us. we can choose to shift the responsibility, or . . . we can choose to shift the paradigm." —bono, rock star and activist

by, children are jumping in and swimming, people are fishing, and everyone is generally having a good time.

You see, we really don't think about water being essential to our lives—water is essential to our fun! Pools, lakes, the beach, water parks . . . water to us means vacation.

I realize I am looking at the lake, that water source, from only one perspective—enjoyment. What if it were my only water source? What if I had to bathe in it, wash my clothes in it, and collect my drinking water from it? I believe my perspective would change.

And maybe that is just what we need. We need to change our perspective on water. We need water to change us.

water for life

Jesus commands us to *"Love your neighbor as yourself."*[91] Some of our neighbors are right across the street, while others are a world away.

Back in that small village in Limones, Guatemala,

every child is still sick because of the water they drink. Every one of them has waterborne parasites. They have food, clothing, and shelter, but they lack the one critical need they cannot live without . . . clean water.

Just down the road a few miles is the last village in Limones. It is called El Rincon de los Limones . . . The End of the Limes. Scattered across a barren looking foothill, this village is home to over 800 families.

Although it's just a short distance from the first village, there is something different in El Rincon and on the faces of the people who call this village home. It is hope. Hope because they have something the other village does not have—clean water.

I was there the day their well was dedicated and used for the first time. The young man who donated the funds to build the well was there too. He had recently received a bonus at work that he could have easily just put in the bank. But when he heard of the desperate need in Guatemala for access to clean water, he thought his funds could be better spent.

He had the honor of cutting the ribbon and praying the dedication prayer for this new well. As we pumped the water out, it was incredible to see the children playing, drinking, and splashing in the clean water. I am sure it is something that young man will never forget. And, I am sure he will never regret using his resources in that way.

El Rincon de los Limones may be at the end . . . but they are no longer living like it. These children will remain healthy because of the clean water. This is the tale of two villages, and the difference is you!

Robert Kennedy once said, "Let no one be discouraged by the belief there is nothing one man or one woman can do against the enormous array of the world's ills—against misery and ignorance, injustice and violence . . . Few will have the greatness to bend history itself; but each of us can work to change a small portion of events, and in the total of all those acts will be written the history of this generation . . ."[92]

Far from the hills of Guatemala, Sentwali used to gather his water from a stream near a rural village in Rwanda. This young boy never knew the water was bad for him, but he did know he was sick often. He knew there were many mosquitoes around the stream, but he didn't know they could harm him.

A clean water well was drilled in his village and now Sentwali, along with his whole village, stays healthy.

It's true that "thousands have lived without love, but none without water," but little Sentwali experienced both.[93] After seeing the dramatic change in his village, he began to trust the men that installed the well and wanted to learn more about them. Sentwali was introduced to the powerful love of Jesus and the Living Water that will never run out, never get dirty, and never be taken away. Sentwali became a Christ follower and is experiencing a total transformation in his life and his community.

Mother Teresa reminded us, "There are no great acts, only small acts done with great love."[94]

It has been said, "Providing access to safe drinking water is one of the most powerful and cost-effective things we can do to save a child's life . . ."[95]

Clean water transforms communities and cultures. Waterborne diseases are drastically reduced.

Countless hours walking to filthy, contaminated ponds are no longer needed. Time spent collecting water is reduced, providing opportunities for women to earn an income and children to receive an education.

Wells bring individuals, families, and communities a better life for today and a better future for tomorrow.

your ticket to change the world

In a recent graduation address, Tom Brokaw challenged the graduates by saying, "You are educated. Your certification is

> "you are educated. your certification is in your degree. you may think of it as the ticket to the good life. let me ask you to think of an alternative. think of it as your ticket to change the world." —tom brokaw

in your degree. You may think of it as the ticket to the good life. Let me ask you to think of an alternative. Think of it as your ticket to change the world."[96]

We each have a ticket to change the world. Some of us have time. Some of us have resources. Some have networks of influence. And others have great passion. We each have a ticket. The question is, what will you do with yours?

It has been said that "the world water crisis is one of the largest public health issues of our time."[97] And today, we have the opportunity to do something about it.

Our vision is to impact 1 million orphaned and disadvantaged children around the world. By providing food, clothing, an education, a loving caregiver, and access to fresh, clean, safe water—we can give them hope.

> unicef reports that the world water crisis is one of the largest public health issues of our time.

If you are like me and you are passionate about making a difference . . . passionate about helping the helpless and giving hope to the hopeless, then I want to challenge you to use your ticket to change the world.

And you can start by saving a child's life.

In a time of crisis and great need, President Jimmy Carter stated, "All of us . . . have an opportunity and an obligation, maybe a duty, to take a portion of our good fortune and invest it in helping others."[98]

What you choose to do today can give a child a life free from disease and full of opportunity. A relatively small amount of money can provide a child, a family, or even an entire community with clean water for the rest of their lives! Can you imagine one gift making that kind of impact?

You can choose to save a life by providing clean water . . . because water changes everything.

Join the cause. cause**life** (www.causelife.org)

do what you can |

"Clean water, the essence of life and a birthright for everyone, must become available to all people now."[99]

—Jean-Michel Cousteau

do

Water equals life . . . causelife is a movement of people dedicated to providing the most essential need to human life—water.   By raising awareness and implementing solutions, causelife provides clean, safe water that changes lives and transforms communities.

| get involved

sponsor a water well

It's amazing what clean water can do to transform a culture. By sponsoring a well, you can provide pure, safe, drinking water for an entire village or community. There are many types of wells . . . from shallow, hand-dug wells, to deep, bore machine-dug wells. Costs vary depending on location and type. To learn more about sponsoring a well, visit causelife.org today.

give water4life

for a child
Six thousand children die every day from preventable

waterborne diseases.[100] These are caused by a contaminated water source. Your donation can give one child
clean, safe, drinking water for 20 years. By providing a
child with water for life, you are giving them a chance at
a better future.

for a family
In communities lacking a nearby water source, wom-
en and children walk several miles to reach a source,
and even then, it's contaminated. Because of this daily
chore, women are unable to provide for their family,
children are unable to attend school, and families suffer.
Your gift can provide clean water for a family of five for 20
years. By giving one family safe drinking water, you can
provide hope and an opportunity for them to thrive in
their community.

become a water activist

voice the cause
Your voice is one of the most important things you
can use to help the cause. By telling others about the
global need for clean water, you can open eyes and

raise awareness. Join our Facebook Cause, follow us on Twitter, check out our YouTube Channel, sign up for our email updates, and invite your family and friends to do the same. There are numerous ways causelife is raising awareness about the need for clean water, and we need your help. Visit causelife.org today and find out how you can become a clean water activist.

host a gathering
Your friends, family, neighbors, and community are your audience, and inviting them into your home is your opportunity. You can host a causelife gathering and help spread the word about the need and the solution. We will make available to you everything you need ... literature, videos, merchandise, and more to make your gathering a success. Visit causelife.org today to learn how you can host a gathering in your home.

sponsor an event
Let's think big! Organize art showings, a Walk for Water or 5k, a golf or tennis tournament, an annual charitable fundraiser. Events are one of the best ways to reach a large audience with the need for clean water. Visit causelife.org today to learn how you can

volunteer, facilitate, or sponsor a causelife event in your community.

sport merchandise
By purchasing and sporting causelife merchandise: water bottles, t-shirts, hats, and more, you not only provide clean water, but you let others know about the need and their chance to participate.

Visit causelife.org today.

what you can do

the authors

vernon brewer

Founder and president of World Help, a nonprofit, humanitarian organization uniquely qualified and strategically positioned to meet the spiritual and physical needs of hurting people around the world. Vernon is also the author of *Forgotten Children: Hungry. Hopeless. Running for their lives.*, *Why? Answers to Weather the Storms of Life.*, *Children of Hope: Be touched. Be inspired. Be changed.*, and *Defining Moments: a journey to the ends of the earth and back.*

noel brewer yeatts

Vice president of World Help and the founder of the Child Sponsorship Program that has provided over 38,000 sponsorships for children in need around the world. Noel is also the co-author of *Children of Hope: Be touched. Be inspired. Be changed.*

dc bowden

Professional writer and photographer. He has traveled extensively, capturing the stories and images of disadvantaged children around the world.

endnotes

introduction

[1]   Robert Redford, as quoted in "Oscilloscope Brings the Award-Winning Water Documentary FLOW : FOR LOVE OF WATER (Environmental News Network, 1 December 2008), http://www.enn.com/press_releases/2737.

[2]   Kimberly Mullen, "Information on Earth's Water" (Westerville, OH: National Ground Water Association, 15 May 2009), http://www.ngwa.org/programs/educator/lessonplans/earthwater.aspx.

[3]   "Where Is Earth's Water Located?" (Washington, DC: United States Geological Survey, 15 May 2009), http://ga.water.usgs.gov/edu/earthwherewater.html.

[4]   "The Water in You" (Washington, DC: United States Geological Survey, 13 May 2009), http://ga.water.usgs.gov/edu/propertyyou.html.

[5]   Bonnie Worthington-Roberts, "Human Nutrition" (Microsoft® Encarta® Online Encyclopedia, 2009), http://encarta.msn.com/encyclopedia_761556865/Human_Nutrition.html.

[6]   Matthew 9:36 (American Standard Version).

water changes children

[7]   "Child Survival Fact Sheet: Water and Sanitation" (New York, NY: United Nations Children's Fund), http://www.unicef.org/media/media_21423.html.

[8]   "Case for Support" (Ottawa, Ontario: Water Can, March 2009), 10, http://www.watercan.com/PDF/Case%20for%20Support_Final_english_2009.pdf.

[9]   Ibid.

[10]   David Redhouse, "No Water, No School," Oasis, Spring/Summer 2004 (London, UK: WaterAid, 2004), 7, http://www.wateraid.org/documents/oasisss04.pdf.

[11]   "To Jump Start Development" State of the World's Children (New York, NY: UNICEF, 2004), 1, http://www.unicef.org/sowc04/files/Chapter1.pdf.

[12]   "The Facts About The Global Drinking Water Crisis" (Redwood City, CA: Blue Planet Run Foundation, 2004), http://blueplanetrun.org/water/facts.

[13]   "WASH Facts and Figures" (Kampala, Uganda: WATSAN Resource Centre), http://www.watsanuganda.watsan.net/page/280.

[14]   "Health and Hygiene Considerations" (New York, NY: Flip Flop Foundation, April 2009), http://www.flipflopfoundation.com/health.html.

[15]   Jenna Klink, "E. Coli Contaminated Drinking Water in Rural Uganda: Using Results to Make an Impact," MINDS@UW (Madison, WI: University of Wisconsin, 2007), http://minds.wisconsin.edu/handle/1793/8130.

cause**life**

water changes health

[16] Kofi Annan, as quoted in "Poverty Biggest Enemy of Health in Developing World, Secretary-General Tells World Health Assembly" (New York, NY: United Nations), http://www.un.org/News/Press/docs/2001/sgsm7808.doc.htm.

[17] "The Environment: Where's the Risk, and Where are Children Safe?" (Science*Daily*, 28 June 2004), http://www.sciencedaily.com/releases/2004/06/040623104827.htm.

[18] Jessica Berman, "WHO: Waterborne Disease is World's Leading Killer" (Washington, DC: Voice of America, 17 March 2005), http://www.voanews.com/english/archive/2005-03/2005-03-17-voa34.cfm.

[19] "Take Action: Protect Our Right to Water. If You Don't Speak Out, Our Access to Clean, Safe, Affordable Water is at Risk." (Washington, DC: Food & Water Watch), http://action.foodandwaterwatch.org/campaign.jsp?campaign_KEY=26890.

[20] "Bacteria" (Science Clarified, 2008), http://www.scienceclarified.com/As-Bi/Bacteria.html.

[21] "Child Survival Fact Sheet: Water and Sanitation," United Nations Children's Fund.

[22] Andrea Gerlin, "A Simple Solution," *Time Online Magazine* (New York, NY: Time Inc., 8 October 2006), http://www.time.com/time/magazine/article/0,9171,1543876,00.html.

[23] Alessandra Marini and Michele Gragnolati, "Malnutrition and Poverty in Guatemala" (Washington, DC: World Bank, January 2003), 3, http://papers.ssrn.com/sol3/papers.cfm?abstract_ID=636329.

[24] "World Bank Policy Research Working Paper 2967," as referenced in Anne Braghetta, "Drawing the Connection between Malnutrition and Lack of Safe Drinking Water in Guatemala" (Franklin, TN: Living Waters for the World), 3, http://www.livingwatersfortheworld.org/docs/drawing-the-connection-en.doc.

[25] "Malaria Facts" (Atlanta, GA: Centers for Disease Control and Prevention, 2007), http://www.cdc.gov/Malaria/facts.htm.

[26] "Water, Sanitation and Hygiene Links to Health" (Geneva, Switzerland: World Health Organization, 2004), http://www.who.int/water_sanitation_health/publications/facts2004/en/.

[27] "Water and Diseases" (Water Missions International, 2006), http://www.watermissions.org/water_diseases.html.

28   "Blinding Disease"(Sheffield, UK: World Mapper, 2006), http://www.
       worldmapper.org/posters/worldmapper_map234_ver5.pdf.
29   "Water Related Diseases" (Geneva, Switzerland: World Health Organization,
       2009), http://www.who.int/water_sanitation_health/diseases/trachoma/en/.
30   "Blinding Disease," World Mapper.
31   "Promoting Health Through Clean Water: Prevention and Treatment of
       Water-Borne Disease" (IHT/Global Health, May 2006), slide 11, http://www.
       sbglobalaction.com/education/Promoting%20Clean%20Water.ppt.
32   Bridget See, "At a Glance: Timor-Leste" (New York, NY: United Nations
       Children's Fund, 17 November 2005), http://www.unicef.org/infobycountry/
       Timorleste_29930.html.
33   "Background Paper on Vaccination Against Typhoid Fever Using New-
       Generation Vaccines" (Typhoid Immunization Working Group, November 2007),
       http://www.who.int/immunization/SAGE_Background_publicpaper_typhoid_
       newVaccines.pdf.
34   "Initiative for Vaccine Research: Typhoid Fever" (Geneva, Switzerland: World
       Health Organization), http://www.who.int/vaccine_research/diseases/typhoid/
       en/.
35   "Initiative for Vaccine Research: Cholera" (Geneva, Switzerland: World Health
       Organization), http://www.who.int/vaccine_research/diseases/diarrhoeal/en/
       index3.html.
36   "Cholera Deaths" (Sheffield, UK: World Mapper, 2006), http://www.
       worldmapper.org/posters/worldmapper_map232_ver5.pdf.
37   "Goal: Reduce Child Mortality" (New York, NY: United Nations Children's Fund),
       http://www.unicef.org/mdg/childmortality.html.
38   "Don't Take on an Empty Stomach: Why HIV Treatment Won't Work Without
       Food" (London, UK: Christian Aid, November 2007), 4, http://www.christianaid.
       org.uk/images/dont_take_on_an_empty_stomach.pdf.

water changes poverty

39   "In-Depth: Running Dry: The Humanitarian Impact of the Global Water Crisis"
       (IRIN: Humanitarian News and Analysis, 2009), http://www.irinnews.org/
       InDepthMain.aspx?InDepthId=13&ReportId=61155.
40   Dr. Wess Stafford, *Too Small to Ignore: Why Children Are the Next Big Thing*
       (Colorado Springs, CO: WaterBrook Press, 2005), 175.

[41] Peter Singer, *The Life You Can Save* (New York, NY: Random House Publishers, 2009), 8.

[42] Robert E. Rector, "How Poor Are America's Poor? Examining the 'Plaque' of Poverty in America" (Washington, DC: The Heritage Foundation, 27 August 2007), http://www.heritage.org/research/welfare/bg2064.cfm.

[43] "New Data Show 1.4 Billion Live on Less Than US $1.25 a Day, But Progress Against Poverty Remains Strong" (Washington, DC: The World Bank, 26 August 2008), http://web.worldbank.org/WBSITE/EXTERNAL/NEWS/0,,contentMDK:218 81954~pagePK:64257043~piPK:437376~theSitePK:4607,00.html.

[44] "Eradication of Poverty," *World Summit for Social Development Copenhagen 1995: Programme of Action of the World Summit for Social Development* (New York, NY: United Nations Department of Economic and Social Affairs: Division for Social Policy and Development, 2008), http://www.un.org/esa/socdev/wssd/pgme_action_ch2.html.

[45] Susan Hunter, *Black Death: AIDS in Africa* (New York, NY: Palgrave MacMillian, 2003), 28.

[46] Luis Bush, *Raising Up a New Generation from the 4/14 Window to Transform the World* (Flushing, NY: Transform World New Generation, 2009), 17.

[47] Shane Claiborne, *The Irresistible Revolution: Living as an Ordinary Radical* (Grand Rapids, MI: Zondervan, 2006), 51.

[48] John Edwards, "The America We Believe In" (Washington, DC: Institute For America's Future, 31 January 2006), http://www.tompaine.com/articles/2006/01/31/the_america_we_believe_in.php.

[49] Claiborne, *The Irresistible Revolution*, 164-165.

[50] Singer, *The Life You Can Save*, 53.

[51] "War and Poverty: What's the Connection?" *Environment Story* (Washington, DC: The World Bank, 9 October 2008), 1, http://youthink.worldbank.org/4teachers/pdf/environment/story-waterandpoverty.pdf.

[52] Kevin Watkins, "Clean Water is a Right but It Also Needs to Have a Price" *International Herald Tribune* (New York, NY: The New York Times Company, 10 November 2006), http://hdr.undp.org/en/reports/global/hdr2006/news/title,199,en.html.

[53] "About MDGs: What They Are" (Millennium Project, 2006), http://www.unmillenniumproject.org/goals/index.htm.

[54] "About MDGs: Goals, Targets and Indicators" (Millennium Project, 2006), http://unmillenniumproject.org/goals/gti.htm.

55   "What is Poverty?" (Milton Keynes, UK: World Vision UK, 2009), 1, http://www.
      worldvision.org.uk/upload/pdf/10_min_Poverty.
56   Paul Slovic, "Numbed By Numbers" *Foreign Policy* (Washington, DC: Slate Group,
      March 2007), http://www.foreignpolicy.com/story/cms.php?story_id=3751.

water changes hunger

57   "Chad-Sudan: Dirty Water, Not Food Shortage, Blamed for Malnutrition Among
      Refugees" (United Nations Office for the Coordination of Humanitarian Affairs
      - Integrated Regional Information Networks [IRIN], 14 July 2004), http://www.
      reliefweb.int/rw/rwb.nsf/AllDocsByUNID/5a9209fce7153de885256ed100697
      a36.
58   "World Bank Policy Research Working Paper 2967," 1.
59   "How Does Safe Water Impact Global Health?" (Geneva, Switzerland: World
      Health Organization, 25 June 2008), http://who.int/features/qa/70/en/index.
      html.
60   "World Bank Policy Research Working Paper 2967," 1.
61   "World Bank Policy Research Working Paper 2967," 3.
62   "Why? Because Hunger Relief in Africa Begins With Water" (Charlotte, NC: The
      Water Project, Inc.), http://thewaterproject.org/hunger.asp.
63   "Sustainable Development and Healthy Environments" (Geneva, Switzerland:
      World Health Organization, 24 September 2004), http://www.searo.who.int/en/
      Section23/Section1326_7472.htm.
64   "The Salt of the Earth: Hazardous for Food Production" (Rome, Italy: Food and
      Agriculture Organization of the United Nations, June 2002), http://www.fao.
      org/worldfoodsummit/english/newsroom/focus/focus1.htm.
65   "Poverty Reduction and Irrigated Agriculture," International Programme for
      Technology and Research in Irrigation and Drainage, Issues Paper No.1 (Rome,
      Italy: Natural Resources Management and Environment Department, January
      1999), 9, ftp://ftp.fao.org/docrep/fao/005/x1000e/x1000e00.pdf.
66   "Micro-Irrigation Technologies" (San Francisco, CA: Kickstart), http://kickstart.
      org/tech/technologies/micro-irrigation.html.
67   "Accumulating Assets Through Animal Agriculture" (Nairobi, Kenya:
      INTERNATIONAL LIVESTOCK RESEARCH INSTITUTE), http://www.ilri.
      org/ILRIPubAware/Uploaded%20Files/2004811933470.01BR_ISS_
      AccumulatingAssetsThroughtAnimalAgriculture.htm.

68   "Facts About Hunger" (Atlanta, GA: CARE USA), http://www.care.org/
       campaigns/world-hunger/facts.asp.
69   "Moving Words: Lao Tzu" (British Broadcasting Corporation), http://www.bbc.
       co.uk/worldservice/learningenglish/movingwords/shortlist/laotzu.shtml.

water changes education

70   Irena Salina, director, *Flow: How Did a Handful of Corporations Steal Our Water?*
       (New York, NY: Oscilloscope Laboratories, 2008).
71   Benjamin Franklin, as quoted in "Facts About Water" (Seattle, WA: Water 1st
       International), 3, http://www.water1st.org/assets/curriculum/water_facts_
       quotes.pdf.
72   Emily Fredrix, "Stricter Labeling Urged for Bottled Water," (New York, NY:
       Associated Press, 8 July 2009), http://hosted.ap.org/dynamic/stories/U/US_
       BOTTLED_WATER_VS_TAP?SITE=TXKER&SECTION=HOME&TEMPLATE=DEFAULT.
73   Salina, *Flow*, 2008.
74   Ibid.
75   "Trick or Treat for UNICEF Tonight, and Help a Deprived Child," *UN News Centre*
       (New York, NY: UN News Service, 31 October 2006), http://www.un.org/apps/
       news/story.asp?NewsID=20429&Cr=unicef&Cr1=.
76   "WASH Facts and Figures," WATSAN Resource Centre.
77   "What We Do: Clean Water Projects" (Santa Rosa, CA: Children's Hunger Relief
       Fund, 2009), http://www.chrf.org/future-clean-water.html.
78   "New Data Show," The World Bank.
79   Redhouse, "No Water, No School," 7.
80   "What We Do: Statistics" (London, UK: WaterAid), http://www.wateraid.org/
       international/what_we_do/statistics/default.asp.
81   "What We Do: Water, Sanitation and Hygiene" (New York, NY: United Nations
       Children's Fund, 22 May 2009), http://www.unicef.org/wash/index_schools.
       html.
82   "Progress Report: Water and Sanitation in Sub-Saharan Africa" (Washington, DC:
       ONE), http://one.org/c/us/progressreport/779/.
83   Stephanie Kinnunen, "Future," *NEED: The Humanitarian Magazine*, Issue 2
       (Minneapolis, MN: NEED Magazine, 2007), 12, http://www.needmagazine.com/
       Issue02/future02.html.

[84]   Nelson Mandela, as quoted in Jone Johnson Lewis, "Education Quotes," *Wisdom Quotes: Quotations to Inspire and Challenge*, http://www.wisdomquotes.com/cat_education.html.

water changes you

[85]   Salina, *Flow*, 2008.
[86]   Singer, *The Life You Can Save*, 3-4.
[87]   "Facts: Water" (Cavelossim, Goa, India: Rehydration Project), http://rehydrate.org/water/index.html.
[88]   Singer, *The Life You Can Save*, 5.
[89]   Jeffrey Sachs, *The End of Poverty: Economic Possibilities for Our Time* (New York, NY: Penguin Group, 2005), Foreword.
[90]   Jan Eliasson and Susan Blumenthal, "Dying for a Drink of Clean Water," *Washington Post*, Section A23 (Washington, DC: The Washington Post Company, 20 September 2005), http://www.washingtonpost.com/wp-dyn/content/article/2005/09/19/AR2005091901295.html.
[91]   Mark 12:31 (New International Version).
[92]   Jeffrey Sachs, *The End of Poverty*, 367-368.
[93]   Salina, *Flow*, 2008.
[94]   "Giving Through Praying" (Teddington, UK: Tearfund, 6 April 2009).
[95]   "What We Do: Clean Water Projects," Children's Hunger Relief Fund.
[96]   Tom Brokaw, as quoted in Robert Consalvo, "Commencement 2008: Faculty Remarks" (Bennington, VT: Southern Vermont College, 2008), https://www.svc.edu/pr/commencement_2008/consalvo_speech.html.
[97]   "The World Water Crisis" (Seattle, WA: Ethos Water), http://ethoswater.com/.
[98]   Jimmy Carter, as quoted in Matthew Pritchard, "Dialogue," *NEED: The Humanitarian Magazine*, Issue 1 (Minneapolis, MN: NEED Magazine, 2006), 125, http://www.needmagazine.com/Issue01/dialogue02.html.
[99]   Jean-Michel Cousteau, "Global Action" (Santa Barbara, CA: Ocean Futures Society, 2007), http://www.oceanfutures.org/global_action.asp.
[100] "Facts: Water," Rehydration Project.